THE ENTRAPRENEUR

A BEGINNER'S GUIDE TO SUCCESS

KEIKO "O.G.KAYKO" THOMAS

Published by:
Penitentiary Rich, LLC
PO BOX 860037
Plano, Tx 75086
www.penitentiaryrich.com

Cover Art - Kince Design Studio:
https://www.instagram.com/kincedesignstudio/

Paperback ISBN: 978-1-7372262-8-4

Printed in the United States of America

First Edition: 2021

DEDICATION

This book is dedicated to all my self made hustlers world-wide. Keep doing you and get this money. Stay focus on your bag,stay away from these suckers, let them see you winning, and never never never give up ever. If you need me to promote your brand or product hit me on social media @o.g.kayko or @penitentiaryrich. Write me @: penitentiary rich,llc - PO BOX 860037-Plano,TX 75086. When I check you out you better be promoting my brand. Its call networking :)
O.G. Kayko

TABLE OF CONTENTS

INTRODUCTION

Dear Readers,

Hello my fellow prisoners, how are you? I hope that all is well and you're doing great under your current circumstances. As you may know by now, I have created this book just for you. The enTRAPrenuew is all about self-help, business, finance, and how-to information. This book is by far hands down the best in its market. Being a rich prisoner isn't just about "money" it's about your mindset as well. I personally know all about trying to make moves from the cell, and the hardships and difficulties that comes with it. Fortunately for me I have succeeded and "now" I am "Penitentiary Rich". I feel as though the biggest measure of success is now about what I have done but what I intend to do for those in the same position as I was. I want to see you "win", I want to see you eat, and I want to see you succeed. My main goal with the enTRAPrenuer is to help and assist you on your path to success from behind the wall. The enTRAPrenuer goals are to inspire, educate, uplift, motivate, and help you on your path to financial freedom. Remember that the one who has the soul of a winner, spirit of a hustler, and motivation to become something greater is already "Penitentiary Rich". Also, remember that time is money and money is time...

Yours Truly,

Keiko "O.G.Kayko" Thomas
Aka The Richest Prisoner

CHAPTER ONE

BANK ACCOUNTS 101

In this chapter, I will be discussing bank accounts and giving you my fellow inmates the breakdown on these different types of accounts. Generally, there are about six types of accounts available for you or your loved ones depending on your needs. Opening a bank account will grant you access to various things like saving your money in a much easier way, buying things from the internet, and many other places. You can open an account online but only if you have access to the right personal information the bank will need to verify your identity. As a rich prisoner, I think that our money in various account will be more pro-active than in our kiosk or prison inmate trust fund that gives us no real interest. With that said, let me put you on game with the six accounts.

1. *Savings Account* – Inmates who want to save money and have it put separately from their day-to-day spending money can use savings accounts. These will have a higher interest rate than checking accounts. But also, you won't be as tempted to spend the money and on top of that it won't be as simple to spend it. This is because you won't get any debit card or checks with this type of account.

***Peep Game* With savings accounts there will be limits on withdraws per month from these accounts. This only applies if you intended to make the transactions within the same month. There are some exceptions when it come special transactions.**

2. *Checking Account* – The most common type of account you will find is going to be a checking account. Basically, they are your typical accounts where

you just save your spending money for most things, whether it's items from a store, online orders or anything of the sort. Your checking account will come with check and a debit card, both will allow you to spend the money in your account.

***Peep Game* Right, so what's actually good about checking accounts is the fact that they don't have a high interest rate on the money you have in your account. The only exceptions will be online accounts or high yield checking accounts. Some accounts will charge maintenance fees monthly if you don't meet certain requirements. If this account earns interest it will be shown as what's called the annual percentage yield (APY) and this includes the interest you earn on interest too, known as compounding.**

- *3. Money Market Accounts* – This type of account is like a mix of both the checking and savings accounts. Known as money market deposit accounts, these also come with checks and a debit card. However, they will also have the six-withdrawal limit that comes with your savings accounts.

*Keep in mind that the difference between your checking or savings and this account is that Money Market Accounts have a much higher interest rate. You may also need a much higher initial deposit which could be anywhere between $2,500 and $25,000. You'll want to have a high daily minimum balance if you want to earn a high interest rate.

- *4. Investment Accounts* – If you're ready to invest in bonds, stocks, or mutual funds then the right way to go is opening a brokerage account.

- *5. Retirement Accounts* – An IRA or Roth IRA are Individual Retirement Accounts that are available to people who want to save money for retirement and are interest in the tax advantages with those accounts.

• *6. Certificate of Deposit* – There is such a thing as a certificate of deposit account, which locks your money up with the financial institution for the term of the deposit agreement. In return, you will get a higher interest rate, if you are going for certificate of deposit accounts with a longer term then you may get a higher rate. Generally, CDs will go from a few months to several years.

***Peep Game* If at any point you need cash from this account, you can withdraw from it but this comes with an early withdraw penalty or fee. You should *NOT* consider this account if you think that you will need cash soon.**

There are multiple types of bank accounts that you can open, where you choose a traditional bank or a credit union to create your new account. Depending on the type that you choose for your money deposits its always important to know that some have higher interest rates while others have more requirements. At the same time, if you withdraw the money from certain types of accounts, you will have to deal with a fee or penalty as a result. So, it's crucial to know what you are dealing with before you make the big step. Hopefully now you will be able to choose the right type of bank account.

Chapter Two

Credit Cards 101

"What are credit cards?" The easiest way to understand credit cards is to think of them as short-term loans that you can use to make all kinds of purchases and, depending on your terms, withdraw cash. Once you've been approved the credit card company will assign your credit limit. Essentially this is the amount of money they allow you to use.

Key Takeaways

Credit cards have a credit limit you can make purchases against and then repay later.

Higher interest rates come with carrying a higher balance

Read all promotional offers closely all the way through the fine print.

Some companies offer rewards programs with things like points, miles, or cash back.

***Peep Game* As you charge things to the card your available credit is reduced, but as you pay back what you spent a portion will go to the interest and the rest will bring your available credit back up.**

To breakdown how credit works, when you use your card to make purchases the card will use a network to process the transaction through your card issuer, who then either approves or declines the transaction based on your available credit limit. Once a transaction is approved, the money is paid out to the merchant and your available credit to spend is reduced by the amount of the purchase. At the end of each billing cycle, you should receive a statement that will tell you all of the transactions for that month along with the previous balance, current balance, the minimum payment, and the due take for this month.

If you pay the balance back in full by the due date then no interest charges are accrued, this Is called the grace period. When you carry a balance from month to month then you will have interest charges being accrued. Credit cards use an annual percentage rate (APR) which includes both your interest rate, annual fees if your card has one, and other costs.

Although the CARD act of 2009 sets strict guidelines on when these companies can or can't raise your rate, most credit cards will have a variable APR which means that your interest rate can change over time.

As a rich prisoner you have to know the difference between your credit card and a debit card. A lot of inmates confuse the two, but I will give you the breakdown between them both.
Credit card vs Debit Card

Although credit cards and debit cards may seem like they're the same, the main difference is that your debit card is spending your money in your checking account but your credit card is taking the money from your available credit limit. When you use your credit limit this means you'll pay it back later with interest, while using your debit card means spending your actual money as soon as the transaction is processed. There is nothing to pay back since the funds were immediately taken at the time of the purchase.

Another difference between credit and debit cards is the impact they have on your credit score. The bank account linked to your debit card isn't going to report your regular bank activity to the credit bureaus, but some credit card companies will use any checking, savings, and physical assets while they approve or deny your credit card application. Opposite of the debit card, your credit card will report your activity to the credit bureaus, and this impacts your

FICO score directly. This score is calculated based on:

- Payment history
- Credit usage
- Credit age
- Credit mix
- Inquiries for new credit

*** Peep Game * When you keep a low balance and make your payments on time then your score will consistently have a positive impact, while maxing out the limits and/or paying later will have negative effects to your overall score and credit history.**

Credit and debit cards are also different because federal law offers more protection against fraud than debit cards. Here is a quick look at each:

Debit Card Liability – If you report unauthorized transactions before the card has been used then you're not responsible.

1. Lost or stolen cards reported within two business days is usually limited to $50 in liability.
2. Lost or stolen cards reported after 2 days but before 60 days of your statement then you're usually limited to $500 in liability.
3. Lost or stolen cards reported more than 60 days after the statement leave you with full liability of all unauthorized transactions.
4. When your physical isn't lost but your information is used to make unauthorized transactions, you have up to 60 days to report it to avoid liability for those unauthorized charges.

Credit Card Liability – Lost or stolen credit cards have a limited liability of $50 under the Fair Credit Billing Act.

How to compare credit cards?

Before you get into looking for your first or next credit card you should compare a few key things about the credit card you're applying for.

- Regular variable APR for purchases
- APR for balance transfers and cash advances
- Promotional APR terms and conditions
- Annual Fees
- Rewards programs
- Introductory bonuses offer terms
- It's also helpful to look at the card's other benefits and features, if any

***Peep Game* Credit cards can be helpful to building your credit if you use them responsibly. Things like paying the bill on time, maintaining a low balance, and only opening credit cards you need can help build and maintain your credit. Also, keep in mind that the best way to avoid interest charges is by paying your credit card bill in full each month.**

Chapter Three

Principal Loan Payouts 101

What is principal? Principal can have many financial meanings, but the most common use refers to the original amount of money that was borrowed in a loan or put into an investment. Other meanings include the face value or a bond or an individual, party of people, the owner of a private company, or the main participant in a transaction.

*** Peep Game * Although 'principal' can have several meanings in the financial and business world, when you're talking about borrowing, principal is the initial size of the bond or loan, which would be paid back. When you're talking about investing then the principal is separate from any earnings or interest, it's the original amount that was used to purchase assets. When you're talking about business, principals are the ones who own a majority or stake in a company, and they usually play a big role in running it. And last, when you're talking about contracts and contractual ventures, principals are the main parties that involved in a transaction and who have rights, duties, and obligations to it.**

Understanding principal - Loans

When you're borrowing, the principal is the size of a loan and can still be the amount owed on a loan. If your mortgage is $100,000 then the principal would be $100,000, but if you paid off $20,000 then you would have a new principal balance of $80,000.

***Peep Game* The principal of the loan will directly affect the amount**

of interest you pay. For instance, if your loan has a principal amount of $10,000 and an annual interest rate of 5% you will have to pay $500 in interest for every year the loan is outstanding.

It's important for you to know that when you're making the monthly payments on a loan, the payment goes to the interest charges first, and after the remainder is goes to the principal. Remember, the amount of interest that you accrue each month can only be reduced by paying down the principal loan.

Understanding Principal - Investing

Principal is also the original amount of investment made in an asset, separate form any earning, or interest accrued. An example would be if you deposited $5,000 into an interest-bearing savings account then at the end of 10 years you will have grown the balance to $6,500. The principal would still be the original $5,000 that you deposited while the remaining $1,500 is considered earnings.

Understanding Principal - Bonds

Bonds have a principal that is the amount of money the issuer of a bond is borrowing and will repay the bondholder in full upon the bond's maturity. Originally when bonds were printed, the amount was printed on the face of the bond which is why the principal can also be known as the "face value" or "par value". The principal of a bond won't include anything extra such as coupons, recurring interest payments, or interest that is accrued (although the issuer is required to pay these). An example is if you have a 10-year bond with recurring $50 coupon payments semiannually then the principal is $10,000 and that is considered separate from the $1,000 worth of coupon payments that would occur over the life of the bond. The bond's principal is only the same as it's market price when it is first issued, and bonds can be purchased for more or less than the principal depending on the state of the bond market at that time.

How does inflation affect principal?

Inflation won't affect the stated value of the principal of a loan, bond, or financial means but it will deteriorate the real value or the principal.

Chapter Four

How to Invest in Stocks

Investing in stocks is a great way to grow your finances by using the power of publicly traded companies. Getting started with investing in stocks can feel challenging despite the long-term potential gains. So, how exactly do you begin to invest in the stock market? Using an online brokerage account to buy stock or stock funds is one of the easiest ways but there is also the option to hire a professional portfolio manager.

***Peep Game* Here is how to get started with investing in stocks even if you don't know that much about investing right now.**

* 5 Easy Steps to get started*

- 1. Decide how you're going to invest
- 2. Open an investment account
- 3. Research and decide what you want to invest in
- 4. Determine how much you're wanting to invest and then buy
- 5. Track your investment portfolio

Bottom Line

The good thing is that investing these days can be done on your own terms even while you're building your knowledge. There are options to do it yourself or have an expert do it for you, whether you're trading actively or investing passively with stocks or stock funds, pick the style of investing that works for you to build your wealth.

CHAPTER FIVE

STOCK MARKET 101

As a prisoner, if the thought of investing your money into the stock market scares you, you are "NOT" alone. Without a lot of experience, a lot of prisoners are concerned because horror stories say the average investor loses 50% of their portfolio's value.

Realistically, investing in the stock market will carry risk, but if you can be disciplined, this is an easy way to build up your net worth. For most people, the value of their home is where most of their net worth is accounted for but the more affluent and richer will generally have more of their wealth invested in stocks.

Key Takeaways
Stocks, or shares of a company, represent ownership equity in the firm, which gives shareholders residual capital gains and dividends on corporate earnings.
Stock markets are where investors come together in a public venue, today this is an electronic marketplace, to buy and sell shares.
Pricing for shares is set by the supply and demand in the market as orders are placed by buyers and sellers. Overflow and bid – Specialists or market makers ensure an orderly and fair market by maintaining spreads.

The definition of a stock, also known as a share or the company's equity, is financial ownership in a company or corporation that equals the claim on the assets (what is owned) and earnings (profits generated).

Owning stock is like having a slice of the company that is equal to the total number of shares and proportionate to the company's overall shares. To break it down, if you own 100,000 shares of a company with 1 million overall shares then you would have 10% ownership stake in it. Typically, companies have millions and billions of outstanding shares

Common and Preferred Stock

When discussing equity you're referring to common shares whose combined market value and trading volume is greater than your preferred shares.

Usually, the difference between common and preferred is that common shares usually have voting rights so the common shareholder will have a say in corporate meetings (like annual general meeting or AGM) – where issues such as election to the board of directors or appointment of an auditor are voted upon, while preferred shares generally don't have voting rights. Preferred shares get their name because they have preference over common shares in the company to receive their dividends and assets in the event the company has a liquidation.

Furthermore, common stock can be classified in terms of voting rights. The basic idea of common shares is they should have one vote per share held, but some companies have dual or multiple classes of their stock who has their own voting rights for each class. An example of the dual class structure would be having Class A and Class B shares. Class A may receive 10 votes per share while the subordinate Class B may only have one vote per share.

Why a Company Issues Shares?

According to Investopedia, corporates top tier likely had their start as a small private entity that had a visionary founder just a few decades ago. For examples you can look at Jack MA who created Alibaba (BABA) in his apartment in

China 1999 or Mark Zuckerberg designing Facebook on his computer from his Harvard dorm room. These two have grown into technology powerhouses within just a couple of decades.

To grow at such a rapid pace, you would need a massive amount of capital. In order to take an idea brewing in your head to an operating company, you'll need to lease an office or factory equipment, hire some employees, buy necessary equipment, buy raw materials, and put in place a sales and distribution network, among other things. Depending on the scale of your business startup you may need a significant amount of capital to acquire these resources.

Raising Capital

Startup companies can use equity financing (selling shares) or debt financing (borrowing money). Debt financing can be a problem for a startup because it may not have many assets to show – especially in businesses such as technology or biotechnology, where a firm has few tangible assets – plus the interest accrued on the loan would be a financial burden in the beginning when a company may not have revenue.

Equity financing is the most common route for a majority of startups who need capital, initially you can source funds from your personal resources such as friends or family to get the business off the ground. As the business expands and capital requirements become more substantial, you can look into angel investors and venture capital firms.

Listing Shares

While a company is establishing themselves, they may need a much larger amount of capital than you could get from your ongoing operations or a bank loan. You can sell shares through an initial public offering (IPO) which will change the status of your company from private with only a few shareholders to a publicly traded company who has numerous members of the public who own shares. An IPO will offer people who invested in the company early a chance to cash out their stake which often brings a handsome reward.

Once a company is publicly trading and listed on the stock exchange the price of shares will fluctuate as their value is reassessed constantly while investors and traders are buying and selling their shares. You can use a lot of ratios and metrics to value stocks, but the most popular method is price/earnings (PE) ration. Also, the analysis of the stock is typically in one of two categories: fundamental analysis or technical analysis.

CHAPTER SIX

HOW TO START A COMPANY

Step One: Choose the right business idea. The first step towards a business ownership is deciding what kind of business to start. Your idea for a small business should be something you're interested in and something that's going to fit your personal goals. This makes you more likely to find success and stay motivated when things may get tough.

Step Two: Plan your business. Successful businesses are built through careful planning. Before you jump into spending money and putting all of your resources toward your business, take some time to critically think about your idea and come up with your game plan.

***Peep Game* Choose a Business Name – What will you name your business? When naming a business, you'll want to choose an available name that follows your states naming rules and resonates with your customers. You can also search Google, GoDaddy, or other websites for available domain names.**

Find a business location – Does your business need a physical location or are you working from home? The location will may have some type of licensing and permits that are required.

Conduct Market Research – Have you thought about who your target market is and gotten to know them? Before you write your business plan, conducting through market research is crucial. This can involve conducting surveys, doing search engine optimization (SEO) research or holding focus groups.

Understanding your target market and analyzing your competitors is essential when writing an effective business plan.

Write a business plan – Have you thought about writing a business plan? While it's helpful to have a business plan to keep things organized, a solid business plan can be used when you're applying for business funding and help you reach those important milestones.

*** Peep Game * I'm going to give you a couple main components to writing a good plan.**

- Product development – What problems does your business solve? How are you setting yourself apart from direct competitors?
- Sales and Marketing – Do you know who your potential buyers are? How do you find these customers and turn them into buyers?
- People and partnerships – What professional relationships will you need to form to be successful? You may have roles to be filled as well.
- Financial Planning – Do you know how many targets or transactions you need to breakeven? It's time to figure out how much money it's going to take to get there and sources you can get the funding from.

Step Three: Get Funding. It's not a secret that businesses need startup funding, but you have to do a couple of things to cover your startup costs first. Start with calculating your businesses costs before seeking outside funding, this is going to help you choose the right resource for funding. The next thing is going to be getting organized with a detailed financial plan for your business.

***Peep Game* Explore Business Funding Options**

Bootstrapping – This is also known as "Do It Yourself" and requires you to

provide the capital you need for your business with your personal savings and current income. When you have things up and running the profit should be reinvested back into the business to continue its growth.
Friends & Family: Financing your business through friends and family loans can be a great way to get the capital you need to start your small business. Mixing business with your friends and family can be aggravating so it's best to establish a written agreement with a repayment plan.
Small business grants – Small business grants are money you apply for through the grantors process and will not have to pay back.
Small Business Loans – You can apply for a small business loan through most banks and lending institutions but it's important to know that this funding method will require repayments, but you would have the startup capital you were looking for.

Step Four: The Business Structure. You'll need to register your company as a legal business entity such as an LLC, Corporation, or Non-Profit.

***Peep Game* Registering your gives you more credibility but also provides protection from personal liability in the event that you get sued. You'll need to do some research to decide which business structure is going to be the right fit for your new business.**

Sole Proprietorship – This is a more informal way to structure your business that isn't incorporate or separated from you.
Partnership – This is also an informal way to structure your business but with multiple owners. They're similar in the fact that they do not have personal liability protection for the owners.
LLCs – This business structure will combine the personal liability protection for your assets that a corporation will along with the flexibility we see in a partnership or sole proprietorship.
Corporations – There are separate legal entities that are owned by sharehold-

ers, like we discussed previously, and these are more attractive to an investor's due to the formal regulations that a corporation will have.
Nonprofits – Nonprofits typically source their funding from donations rather than investors and are usually created to further a social cause. This business structure has a distinct benefit of being exempt from paying taxes.

***Peep Game* If you still don't want to register your business as a legal entity then you will be held personally responsible for all debts and liabilities associated with your business.**

Step Five: Forming the business. By now you should have chosen a business structure so the next step would be to form your business. Regardless of your chosen structure, these next few steps are common for each:

- Name your business
- Every business needs a representative to handle/accept tax documents for your business, this is called your registered agent.
- The IRS will assign you an Employer Identification Number (EIN)
- Each business structure will have formation documents to file with the state.

Each business structure will have its own requirements that are unique from the others so you could form your business yourself or hire a professional service to form your business. The steps below breakdown this process for each business structure.

LLC – These are your simplest business structure to formally create and maintain. They have less paperwork than the other business structure and can be formed with the following steps:

- Choose the state of your LLC
- Provide the name you've picked for your business
- Pick your registered agent
- File your states required paperwork for an LLC
- Put together an operating agreement for your LLC
- Obtain your EIN number

Corporation - To start your business as a corporation you're going to have to decide the type of your corporation, like a C corporation, S corporation, or B corporation. These are the steps to form a corporation:

- Provide the name you've picked for your corporation
- Pick your registered agent
- Have an organizational meeting
- File the formation documents with your state
- Obtain your EIN number

Nonprofit - If forming a Nonprofit is the best business structure for you then you'll follow some of the same steps as the corporation or LLC. However, an additional step in this process is applying for tax exemption, otherwise known as 501(c)(3), through the IRS.

- Provide the name of your nonprofit
- Pick your registered agent
- Determine your board members and officers
- Acquire bylaws and a conflict-of-interest policy.
- File your articles of incorporation
- Obtain your EIN
- Apply for the 501(c)(3)

Step Six: Now that you have a formal business structure, it's time to open a business bank account, credit cards, and accounting that is dedicated to the business. This is how you're going to protect your personal assets.

***Peep Game* In the event that your business gets sued, having your personal and business accounts mixed will put your personal assets at risk. The legal term used when this happens is "piercing the corporate veil."**

Here are some steps to protect your business:
1. Start with a business bank accounts! This is the first separation of your personal and company assets, which is necessary to protect your personal assets.
2. Getting a business credit card: Helps you separate personal and business expenses and build your company's credit history, which can be useful to raise capital later on.
3. Setup a business accounting system that helps you track your business and keeps your annual tax filing simple. Some accounting software will let your download your bank and credit card transactions to keep things fast and easy.

***Peep Game* You can hire a business accountant to help you navigate all your business accounting and tax needs from payroll to sales tax**

Step Seven: Get insured. Business insurance helps you focus on your growing business by managing risks. Your three most common types to consider are:

1. General Liability Insurance
2. Workers Compensation Insurance
3. Professional Liability Insurance

Step Eight: Look into your federal, state and local government laws and regulations that may require you to obtain some permits and/or licensing.

Step Nine: Unless you're planning to be your only employee, now would be the time to hire a team that can help your build a successful business.

Step Ten: Some of the most memorable businesses are defined by their branding and logo.

Step Eleven: Now that you have a logo and brand, the next step will be to establish your business's website.

Step Twelve: Promote and market your business. Some of the most common and effective methods to promoting your business are:

- Press releases
- Facebook
- YouTube
- Google my business

CHAPTER SEVEN

How to get funding for a business (8 ways)

1. Beginning with bootstrapping.

In the beginning, many entrepreneurs will choose bootstrapping when they're starting out, which will use their personal funds, assets, or even any home equity lines that may be available.

2. Consider friends and family

Asking your friends and family for money might seem a little challenging, but asking those closest to you is often a good first step before getting external funding, and it can't hurt to ask.

*** Peep Game* Before you ask your friends and family for money though you should have a business plan ready.**

3. Explore alternative funding sources

If you're looking for a relatively small amount of money (anywhere from $25 - $5,000) there are quite a few micro-loan organizations that lend to startups and entrepreneurs such as Kiva and Accion. These websites cater to low-income entrepreneurs in the US or those working for social good. Many people like to use crowdfunding with websites such as Kickstarter and Indiegogo.

4. Look Local

Check out your local small business development center to see what assistance and networking may be offered.

5. Consider taking out loans

If you can show that you've starting making money then you could consider applying for small business loans.

6. Look to angels

If you have a tech start-up, you'll eventually need more capital to really get going – to hire people or get office space. Sometimes established business professionals who has high networks are looking to invest in promising companies, these are called angel investors and can be a good place to start.

7. Venture Capitalist

If you're looking for some serious funding (at least $1 million). You'll need to turn to venture capital. (VCs) will give you larger amounts of money but they're looking for thorough business plan.

8. Ready to launch

Finding funding can be the hardest part of getting your business off the ground but also the most regarding.

Chapter Eight

30 Ways to Market and Promote

1. Create and verify your google business profile.
2. Get a website.
3. Implement search engine optimization
4. Create a business blog
5. Share your content
6. Run Google Ads
7. Create listing on the major directories
8. Optimize your listings
9. Get online customer reviews
10. Monitor and respond to reviews
11. Prioritize Facebook
12. Connect and contribute on linked in
13. Upload Videos to Youtube
14. Advertise on Youtube
15. Engage your audience on Instagram
16. Share on Twitter
17. Give Pinterest a shot
18. Try out Tik Tok
19. Join Online Communities
20. Try an influencer marketing collaboration
21. Invest in social media advertising
22. Strive to get local press

23. Form Partnerships
24. Network, network, network
25. Attend, host, or sponsor local events
26. Try out direct mail
27. Advertise locally and offline
28. Attend trade shows
29. Run email marketing campaigns
30. Make advocates out of your employees.

Chapter Nine

12 Leadership Skills

1. Taking initiative

Most bosses are only going to assign you tasks that they know you can do so to learn things outside of your primary knowledge, you'll want to volunteer to take on more responsibilities. Focus on learning new competencies that will take you above and beyond your current position.

2. Don't be complacent.

When you step out of your comfort zone and challenge yourself to improve the more, you're learning as you work. Taking on more responsibilities shows you can take initiative, which will only help move you into a leadership role at your workplace. When that day comes, your newfound knowledge for making improvements will help others accept you as a leader easier.

3. Critical Thinking

In a more high-profile job, you have to apply more critical thinking to a situation so you can foresee and prevent potential problems in the workplace.

4 Listening Effectively

When you're a leader you're frequently speaking in front of the team, coming up with business strategies, and communicating with clients and employees. Listening skills are one of the most important skills of a leader and without this you will miss out on key information such as feedback from your team and clients. To actively listen you will need to maintain eye contact, avoid distractions, and respond appropriately.

5.Feedback is key

In any verbal communication you should be aware of body languages and gestures to decipher what people are really saying. If you're actively listening, then you can pick up feedback from more than what is said.

6. Motivate others

A true leader has a positively influence on their people and they can energize and motivate their team when they may lose their passion and ambitions. A good leader seeks out their team members to find out what they need and want. How does a leader motivate people? They use active listening to analyze and respond in a way that will empower them to be more involved in the process. Some reasons employees lost motivation and ambition include them being tired of repetitive tasks, they're facing some difficulties, or they may be disappointed they're not being asked to get more involved.

7. Creating a positive work environment

Maintaining a positive work environment is essential to motivating your team. You can provide lunch or snacks and treats to unwind and feel appreciated, this is a positive way to reward hitting benchmarks.

8. Discipline

In order to effectively accomplish all of the tasks in your vision or goals, you'll need discipline. This is required if you want to effectively execute your idea.

9. Constant Learning

Leadership and learning are essential to one another. With things changing so rapidly it is important to constantly be learning and challenging yourself. By studying other leaders, you can incorporate some of their qualities such as their mannerisms and the way they communicate into your leadership style.

10. Know how to delegate

Successful leaders don't micromanage, they delegate work to their employees which makes them feel more empowered and have more opportunities to learn a new skill. By delegating to your team, this allows you to achieve the goals you have for yourself but if you're a project leader you're still responsible for the work in the end. This is why it's important for leaders to assign tasks based on who has the skills to complete them. By having clear roles, responsibilities, and deadlines you can delegate and get the project completed.

11. Handling Conflicts

Leaders sometimes have to have the courage to speak up to an employee that may come in with a negative attitude or doesn't work to their full ability. These situations require you to be straightforward and honest in a private conversation to address the issue.

12. Be a follower

As a good leader, you should recognize the value in learning from your team and encouraging others to learn from them. This can help you and others learn more from someone who specializes in a certain area. You should instill confidence in your employees by encouraging their new ideas and giving them confidence.

*** Peep Game * Good Leadership skills are essential to career development. If you're looking to improve your leadership skills you'll want to consider how you can be more influential and if you're already a leader you should think about how you can influence others.**

CHAPTER TEN

ABCS ON TIME MANAGEMENT

Time management, by definition, is the proves of controlling your time spent on specific activities in order to increase your productivity, effectiveness, and how efficient you are. This puts various demands on someone with their social life, family, personal interests and hobbies. Using your time effectively will give you the choice on spending or managing your activities at your own time and pace. To be more successful at improving time management you can apply a range of skills, tools, and techniques to accomplish projects and goals within the due date. On any project, initially time management is necessary to determine the completion time and scope of your project, but you should also know that technical and structural differences exist in time management because of a variety of cultural concepts of time. Recurring themes that show through literature are:

- Consider the cost benefit, quality of your results, and time to complete a task or project to create an environment that promotes effectiveness.
- Set your priorities
- Reduce your time that is spent on non-priorities
- Set up and execute your goals
- Cultural views on time management can affect the way people manage their time.

To break this down, viewing time in a linear way means you view it as flowing from one moment to the next in a linear fashion, which is the most common perception in America along with most Northern European countries like Switzerland, Germany, and England. In these places, people tend to place more importance on productive time management and they typically avoid decisions that would result in wasting time. Generally speaking, these cultures prefer to do things one at a time to accomplish a task with better focus and more productive time management.

Creating an Effective Environment

You should stress tasks related to creating an environment that you feel gives you "real" effectiveness. Some strategies to achieve this are:

- Get organized – taking note of any paperwork and tasks
- Protecting your time – by insulation, isolation, and delegation
- Emphasize achievements from goal management and focus, with motivational emphasis.
- Recovering from bad time- habits – recover from underlying psychological problems, for example, procrastination.

Timing your tasks is also important to overcoming psychological issues such as procrastination. Often your tasks that require more concentration and energy should be performed in the beginning of the day when you're more refreshed.

Setting priorities and goals

Strategies that are recommended when managing your time are:

- Set goals and prioritize the order you're working
- Set some gravitational goals – these attract actions automatically.

ABCD analysis

Categorizing larger data into groups is a technique that businesses have used for a long time. These groups are often marked A, B, C, D hence the names. Here is how you rank activities:

A – Tasks that are recognized as being urgent and important
B – Tasks that are important but they're not urgent
C – Tasks that are urgent but are not important
D – Tasks that are not urgent or important
Each group is then ranked – ordered by priority

- Define your life by your goals and prioritizes your goals
- To be successful you have to keep things you regularly need to accomplish organized
- Streamline things you may not like to do, but have to do
- Conserve things you should do or may even like to do, but they are not pressing or urgent
- Pay attention to the remaining things that may make a difference

Elimination of non-priorities
Eliminating tasks that aren't valuable to you or the organization are also covered in time management skills.

CHAPTER ELEVEN

10 REASONS WHY SMALL BUSINESSES FAIL

10. No business plan or poor planning
9. Failure to understand customer behavior
8. Inventory mismanagement
7. Unsustainable Growth
6. Lack of Sales
5. Trying to do it all
4. Underestimating administrative tasks
3. Refusal to pivot
2. Lack of data
1. Poor management

***Peep Game *These ten reasons should give you a solid understanding of how to turn around a failing small business, so your company doesn't become a failure rate statistic. You can't avoid all of these reasons but you can be aware and think ahead about what you can do to overcome each and still come out winning.**

CHAPTER TWELVE

25 DO'S AND DON'TS TO MAKE YOUR BUSINESS PROFITABLE

How to make profit in your small business:

1. Do determine the precise cost for your business.
Before you can work on increasing your profits you should know where you're starting at after adding up all of your costs. To come up with this number you'll need to think about general expenses and how much your regular activities are.

2. Don't waste time on activities that aren't valuable.
Once you know the value of your time, you can focus more of your time on things that push results for your business and get rid of the things that aren't adding value to your business.

3. Do automate your process where possible.
Most of your day-to-day activities can be considered low value and are easily accomplished through automated software and online solutions. This accomplishes basic functions while not spending a lot of time to do so.

4. Don't use a paper system.
Relying on paper can be an inefficient in the sense that paper can get misplaced and end up costing more than using online tools or software. When you use automated systems, this will eliminate waste, when possible, in terms of expenses.
5. Do track and analyze your time spent.
Find a way that you can track your time so you can get a good picture of

where your time is being spent and see where you can knock out other wastes in your business.

6. Don't forget to consider how your employees spend their time.
Potentially, there is tons of wasted when you analyze how your time is spending their time and you will need to be looking for ways to track and hold people accountable.

7. Do keep track of the finances regularly.
Now that you have a way that you're tracking your time, expenses and earnings, you can keep a close eye on those things regularly. This can help you make decisions about what is successful and what needs work.

8. Don't underprice your business.
Frequently, businesses are making low profits because they're undercharging the customers. If you're barely coving the expenses, then this is a good time to look into a more sustainable offering and cut waste where you can.

9. Do keep the buying process as easy as possible.
Don't make your customers have to jump through hoops to complete their purchase, potential roadblocks during their purchase process could drive them to look for a competitor instead.

10. Don't make bringing in new customers your primary focus.
While new customers are always welcome, they shouldn't cause you to stop trying to increase sales with your current existing customers.

11. Do your best to try and prevent theft and waste.
Every business will have theft and waste most likely, but you should always have systems in place to detect and alert you of any irregularities as soon as possible.

12. Don't provide constant discounting to try and drive sales.
You may occasionally offer discounts as a strategy to move inventory or attract new customers but always having a discount will devalue your product or service.

13. Do consider providing bulk discounts.
Bulk discounts can increase sales and traffic by bunding or a similar offer that's purpose is to increase the size of the customer's order. This would provide a discount to the customer but only if they purchase the bulk amount, which brings in more money to the company overall.

14. Don't hold onto excess inventory.
Another benefit of using a bulk discount or incentive is moving excess product that is costing you money to manage and store.

15. Do prioritize your top sellers.
When your business is actually selling products then it makes sense to put your top sellers on big new opportunities or prospects. Using these people give you the best chance of closing the sale.

16. Don't keep track of supplier costs.
You can't control the price of a vendor or supplier, but you can keep track of those prices because they change constantly, and this is the only way to be sure you're always getting the best price.

17. Do negotiate with vendors.
Vendors can sometimes have excessive pricing so before you just pay full price for your order, it's not a bad idea to try and negotiate a lower cost.

18. Don't continue to pay for expensive services or activities.
You may decide that what certain vendors provide is not worth the cost and

therefore need to be cut out of the budget. Analyze the cost and benefit of these to stay on top of the extra expenses.

19. Do confirm your service appointments.

You can waste a lot of time showing up to a service call where the customer isn't actually home so it's always best practice to call and confirm the appointment before you waste time and resources showing up.

20. Don't underrate your time.

Just as I said with products, undercharging for services can sometimes bring down profits because you're not valuing your time as you should. You need to consider every part of the process from the parts to the administrative work that would be involved.

21. Do put focus on consistently providing good customer service.

Regardless of the product or service that you offer, giving the customer a great experience should always be at the top of your priorities. Good customer service can drive referrals and repeat business, which you can think about as free marketing.

22. Don't continue putting money into marking that isn't working.

Marketing is going to be one of the biggest expenses in your business and it can be worth it in some cases. But you have to keep track of each tactic to determine which is providing results and which is probably best to cut off.

23. Do keep track of everything.

I mean everything from suppliers to marketing, you should always re-evaluate and keep track of what costs are really worth it and working for your business. Then you need to cut ties with the rest.

24. Don't chase everything that sounds exciting.

When you're considering new opportunities to grow your business, carefully consider and research the risk and reward around that new opportunity before spending time and resources on something that doesn't work.

25. Do focus on the overall view of your business.

Now that you've made your business more efficient in its costs and day to day operations, you can focus on the overall picture of what's going on in your business and what it takes to be successful.

Chapter Thirteen

How to open a liquor store – 5 steps

1. Write a business plan.

Liquor stores can be very difficult to start and keep running so before you set up your business, you're going to want to do your due diligence by researching and coming up with a business plan. Of course, these same challenges can be much easier if you're purchasing a liquor store that is already doing well.

2. Choose your ideal location to rent or buy.

If you're buying an established store instead of opening one on your own, then you're going to need to locate a store that is within your price range and for sale. Keep in mind the better shape the business is in the better chance you have at getting a loan to buy the business.

3. Secure the necessary funding.

It's very likely that you're going to need a business loan to be able to buy an existing liquor store or open one of your own. You will need enough to cover the funds to buy the business, the supply, and/or location, and the cost to keeping things running once you've opened, which can be more expensive.

4. Register your business.

Now that you have a business plan, location and funding, it's time to register your business as a legal business entity with the name you have chosen. Before you get to this step you need to verify the name you want is available.

5. Get licenses, permits and insurance.

To legally operate your liquor store, you're going to need to obtain the licenses, permits, and insurance necessary. This is with any business although I know your dreams of opening or buying a liquor store probably don't start with a long trail of applications.

***Peep Game*The cost of liquor licenses varies by state and as you can guess, they can go well into the tens (of hundreds) or thousands of dollars. To add to the licensing headache, every city, county, and state has a different set of rules and laws, you can see which department you're working with for your business. Keep in mind, depending on your state and whether it has blue laws, you might not be able to sell alcohol before a certain time of day or on certain days of the week, like Sundays.**

Chapter Fourteen

How to Open a Landscaping Business

Start by choosing the services you want to provide, you'll have to put together the necessary landscaping equipment, which you can rent or buy if you choose. Once you know the equipment that you're going to need then you can compare the option to buy things outright or if it's a cheaper option to rent.

Before you're taking clients, you're going to want to have the required business license, licenses, and EIN, in addition to any necessary business insurance policies. General liability insurance is the most important and it covers everything from accidental repairs to legal fees and damages that need to be paid out. Accidents will happen, so if you ran over a sprinkler head or caused damage, you'll want to be covered when they do.

A second insurance you'll want to obtain is employment law liability insurance. This will cover you if you were to miscalculate overtime or have wage and hours violations. You're going to want this insurance before you scale your business up and take on more employees.

*** Peep Game * Many small business owners will go it alone in the beginning without an account or attorney. Considering the unpredictability of the future of overtime wages, this insurance could save your business.**

Set your pricing and strategize your marketing plan. Here you can start with

Facebook, Instagram, and other social media and SEO tactics to increase your visibility on search engines like Google.

While you're starting up, you're landscaping business it's important that you keep your finances on track. You may not want to rely on pen and paper for this either, with automated software's like QuickBooks, even a spreadsheet is an outdated method.

The economics of starting a landscaping business is that most lawn care operators will make around $30-$50 per hour. If you have the ambition to go further and you can apply your work ethic, dedication, people skills, and willingness to learn things such as management and marketing software, then you have little stopping you from owning your own landscaping business.

Chapter Fifteen

How to Make a Movie

Some first-time filmmakers, or if you're shooting with a low budget, find it useful to produce their films outside of a traditional studio system. Independent films, also known as, "indie films", give the creator more control of the content, voice, and style of their film. Basically, when you don't have a big budget you'll have less crew members, this can make you more hands on with your film and gives you more freedom to tell the story how you want.

What is an indie film?
Films that aren't made with a major production company or studio are considered indie films, they can be feature length or short films. These films often have lower budgets that range from a few thousand dollars to a few million.

What to consider before making an indie film?
The script. It doesn't matter if you're looking for a film to produce or working on a story yourself, it's all going to start with the script. Even though you have more control over the film than you would in a studio, you can't just make any movie. It's not likely that you're going to start out with big special effects, traveling to multiple locations, or using a lot of computer-generated imagery, also called CGI.

The production budgets. Do you know how much money you need to get your film made? Do you have any funds to personally contribute and how much will you then need to raise? Maybe you've found a financial producer or an independent studio that's willing to chip in, but otherwise you're going to have to find a way to secure the funds. After you've considered all of your costs, including pre-production, production insurance, and postproduction, you'll want to consider all of your fundraising options from asking your family and friends to looking into crowdfunding sites such as Kickstarter and IndieGoGo.

Your Cast. Studios like to rely on big name actors for their films to market the film to their audience but these big-name actors cost money. You should carefully weigh different casting opportunities and don't spend too much on a small roll just because you're hoping their name will give the film a boost. If you're prepared to go searching in places like improv clubs, storytelling events, or open casting calls in person or online. There are plenty of talented actors that will raise the bar for the rest of the cast without breaking the budget.

How to make an indie movie?

Since you won't have the same resources as a Hollywood studio, most of their roles will fall to you and your limited crew, which makes the whole process more hands on than a Hollywood film. There's no specific way to making an indie movie, here's a general guideline you can use:

Find your script. It all starts with a script regardless of the budget but working with a low-budget production means you have to carefully consider your creative choices to make sure the concept fits the budget. Films with special effects, intense makeup or many backgrounds aren't likely to be the best choice for your first or an independent film. When you take into consideration things like the genre, number of characters, and the setting you can tell a more cost-effective story in the long run.

Sort your budget. Now that you have your story it's time to breakdown how much it's going to cost. You're still going to have to work with some experienced people throughout the filmmaking process but knowing how much you need to be spending on each department will keep tracking your finances easier and keep you within your budget.

Hire your crew. Start with your most important roles of the production and fill them first. For example, an experienced cinematographer who can understand your vision, especially as a first-time director, is important to increasing the production value and saving your time so you can focus on other responsibilities. Cinematographers are also known as the director of photography, or DP, and they can be in charge of things like cameras, lighting, and other important technical aspects.

Get your cast. You can use many types of low budget agreements for SAG eligible actors but keep in mind these costs can add up. According to the SAG-AFTRA low budget criteria, there's a current day rate of $125. This may not seem like a lot but if you shoot for eight days, you'll have spent $1,000 and still need to pay for any other actors as well. It's also a good idea to consider contingency funds for things like overtime.

Prep your shoot days. Keep a production bible with all of the necessary information for your shoot, including a contingency plan, such as your shot list, scene layouts and character notes. Prepare for setbacks, all productions have them, whether you lose a location or deal with inclement weather, try to use the natural element to your advantage when you can. Taking a worst-case scenario and turning it to work in your favor can mean using an actual rainstorm to film your scene instead of staging your weather conditions with expensive equipment that produces rain.

Mind the post productions. Your editor can take a good film and turn it into a great film, and now that you've shot and edited your film, it's time to debut it to the world. Using festivals such as Sundance or SXSW can require money for travel, but these are the bigger festivals, and they can lead to securing a film distributor who is going to help you finally have the audience for your indie film.

CHAPTER SIXTEEN

HOW TO START A BARBERSHOP

Going independent?
Looking to establish your own barbershop? For a lot of barbers in the industry, having your own independent barbershop is the ultimate dream. This lets you express your creative talents as an independent craftsperson and artist. Go out to international barbering events, network with your own business cards, and eventually develop a clientele that flies to see you.

Barbering as a business
As an up and coming professional, opening your own barbershop is an exciting investment you're making in your future, but you should also be prepared to make a significant personal investment. Putting down a large chunk of change can cover things like a building lease, equipment, inventory, and supplies to cover your waiting room, breakroom, and barbering areas. Barbering is an aesthetic trade so it's very important that the inside of the shop looks impeccable.

*** Peep Game * While you're on this path of opening your own barbershop, consider the words barbershop and business separate and take the time to understand both aspects in great detail.**

Start by making a business plan
Sit down and figure out all of your expenses including startup costs and recurring operating costs on a monthly and yearly basis. Having these numbers can help you figure out how many clients you need to see per day/week to

meet or exceed your expenses to make a profit.

***Peep Game* You're going to need at least $5,000-$10,000 to get started depending on costs in your area and the supplies you need to get started. You can either save up for your initial investment or look into a bank loan but if you're looking to go the route of a bank loan then you'd better develop a very solid business plan to show them.**

Legal Consideration

Make sure you're operating legally by being aware of all of the laws in your jurisdiction including employment, business, and tax laws for your city, county, and state, as well as any federal regulations.

Getting a city or county business license

You can obtain a business license through your county or city's business department, and this process is easier than you may think, with usually only a one-to-two-page application. Before you go to apply for a business license though, you'll need to know what type of business you want to form. If you're forming anything beyond a sole proprietorship, and sometimes those too, you'll want to consult with an accountant.

Sole Proprietor

This model is if you don't have any employees and plan to be the sole owner and operator of your barbershop, essentially doing everything.

LLC – Limited Liability Company

This is the model you would use if you're planning to be a main boss and hire employees. On tax filings you can report earnings as personal income but also maintain the layer of protection from things like lawsuits. If you 're considering purchasing a franchise such as Supercuts or Sports Clips you may want to use this option as well.

Corporation
This is the model you would use if you're planning to open a large barbershop business with many employees and attracting investors.
Since we're talking about licensing, there's a good chance you're going to be required to hold liability insurance along with your business license. Even if this isn't required, you should carefully consider liability and business insurance.

Meeting State Board Requirements
State board requirements for barbering/cosmetology can be challenging and will differ from state to stat but you can always find your local jurisdictions requirements by checking out the states local board. Often this board is working with your local health department to conduct the inspections and ensure you, and others, are in compliance with any and all state regulations.

- Completed independent barbershop owner application
- Proof that you own or lease the business address
- Proof of a city or county business licensed barber.
- Facility requirements like:
    1. Hot and Cold water
    2. Public Bathrooms
    3. Drinking Water

Each barber chair may have a square footage requirement (such as 35 square feet per chair)
Containers for trash and soiled items
Cabinets that close for storage or barbering tools and clean towels

***Peep Game* Depending on the conditioner of your barbershop when you've purchased or leased it, meeting your states requirements could involve renovations, designs by an architect, and various plumbing, electrical, and occupancy inspections. I don't say all of this to discourage you but to encourage you to research your local requirements so you**

can price these out and know how much your investing. These things should all be taken into consideration when you develop a business plan.

Consider when Hiring Employees: Renting Chairs, Commission, and Salary. As a general rule, it's said that if you can't pay the rent yourself then don't open a barbershop but once you've successfully opened and established your shop, it's time to consider hiring employees.

***Peep Game* When you're thinking about hiring employees, consider all of your options for salary, commission, or booth/chair renting. The rules around each of these employment regulations will vary by state so you'll want to make sure that you're aware of any state and tax obligations. You can find out exactly what you need to do by looking into your local board.**

Salary/Wage/Commission

By choosing to go the route of a salary, hourly wage, or commission you're building an environment that isn't competitive. While other arrangements could lead to arguments over whose clients are whose, this setup will bring your employees together to give walk-ins the shave of their lives. Overall, this arrangement will leave you very involved in the daily operations including marketing and advertising your services and promotions.

Renting Barber Chairs/Booths

Renting out your chairs, or "booths", is a more hands off approach to your barbershop. This provides a fixed guarantee on the amount of income you're receiving from your tenants and provides you with more time to focus on your own clients. Ideally, you build a sense of camaraderie with your tenants who are working on clients next to you.

Combination Chair Rental and Commission

A combination of chair rental and commission based is an approach that would provide your employees with the most working options. While this may be a headache for you come tax time, this will more likely result in happy employees or chair renters who will choose to stay at your shop longer.

Barber Business Bookkeeping

You're going to need to file your business taxes at a minimum of once per year, in some states it is quarterly, and this is where your detailed financial records come into action. You should consider hiring an account for this, especially for the first couple of years, to ensure things are filed correctly if you're running anything more than a sole proprietorship but even many of those will hire an accountant.

***Peep Game* Pay attention to how the IRS classifies your employment arrangement, independent contractor or employee, which can vary between states. The IRS could consider barbers who work on commission with their own clients' tools to be your employees.**

CHAPTER SEVENTEEN

HOW TO OWN A TRUCKING COMPANY – 9 STEPS

1) Get your CDL and driving experience

First things first, you need to obtain a commercial driver's license (CDL). To get this accomplished you can attend a private truck driving school, but some companies have their own programs, or they will sponsor you to go to school for a CDL. Many of the drivers who go on to become owner-operators will get their start in the business by serving as company drivers for the first few years.

2) Develop a solid business plan

While you're preparing to start your business, you're going to have to make sure you have a business plan. This should detail out specific projections for revenue and expenses, including money that you use to pay yourself for living expenses. This may be something you want to hire a business advisor to help you determine what makes the most sense.

3) Determine how to structure your business

Common structures of trucking business include:

- Sole Proprietorship
- Partnership
- Limited Liability Company (LLC)
- Corporation (C-Corp; S-Corp; etc.)

* Each of these business structures have their own advantages and disadvantages that are mostly related to liability and taxes. To find out which one of these is best suited for you it's probably best to meet with an accountant.

4. Gather money to cover startup costs

There is a big investment up front to start a trucking business mainly due to purchasing a tractor and trailed, plus any licensing and registrations you may be required to have. It's recommended to have at least six months of your operation in saving to cover things such as your lease payments if you decide to finance your equipment.

5. Plan out your ongoing business operations

Strategize how your business will operate all the way down to small, but important, issues such as:

- Operations: Where do you park your truck/equipment and who is going to maintain it?
- Sales: Where are you finding loads?
- Back Office: How do you plan to handle things like invoicing, payroll, accounting, and taxes?

6. Ensure compliance with federal and state government regulations

You need to comply with the following before you can begin operating:

- USDOT Number: The US Department of Transportation (DOT) issues a unique identifier that carriers are required to have. These numbers are used to collect and monitor several things such as safety information, inspections, or crash investigations.

- Operations Authority – DOT dictates the type of loads you can carry, all for-hire carriers have to have operating authority from DOT
- Heavy vehicles use tax – the federal government is charging an annual tax on trucks exceeding 55,000 pounds to fund highway programs
- Internal Registration plan (IRP) – You'll want to contact your states transportation website to register but the IRP distributes registration fees that are based on the distance traveled in each state or Canadian providence.
- International Fuel Tax Agreement (IFTA) – Carrier's file quarterly fuel tax

reports that determine their tax and distributes it to the states. The lower 48 states and Canadian providences simplify the reporting of fuel across state lines by having established the IFTA

- BOC – 3 filing – all carriers have to have a process agent who can receive court papers that may be served in a legal filing. You will need to designate a process agent in each state when you have an established office or contracts. Some companies do offer a more blanket coverage that will designate your process agent in every US state.
- Drug Testing and FMCSA Clearinghouse – To stay legal, manage your program that tests for drugs and register all of your drivers with the FMCSA clearinghouse. Other state or federal regulations will need to be considered as well such as weight and size standards, EPA/Air Quality regulations, and safety rules. You can get a list of regulations and safety rules from the US small business administration. DAT authority can help with your IFTA reporting and compliance requirements if you need someone else to handle the paperwork.

7. Research and obtain proper insurance coverages

A significant expense to consider with your freight transportation company is types of insurance you could be required to have, which include:

- Primary Liability: In case of an accident where you are at fault, $750,000 in primary liability coverage is required but many shippers or brokers require at least $1 million in liability coverage.
- Cargo: This covers damage to the freight or theft, depending on what you're hauling this is commonly $100,000 to cover cargo.
- Physical Damage: This will cover the truck in accidents where you are not liable
- Non – Trucking – Use (bobtail): This covers liability for an accident while you are not hauling for someone else.
- Per load insurance: you can cut you annualized insurance costs and even cover specialty loads with all-risk smart coverage that is cost-effective and can

be found in fewer than 40 seconds.

8. Decide to buy or lease your truck and trailer.

This is the same with purchasing vehicles, you can lease or purchase your equipment outright but either way you need to know what type of freight you plan to carry. Do you plan to sleep in the cabin for long trips or do you plan to only run day trips? You'll have options such as a van, refrigerated trailer, or a flatbed and below you'll see some of the common types of leases.

- Operating (full-service) lease: Under an operating lease you're responsible for the maintenance, taxes, permits, but at the end of the lease term you walk away.
- Terminal Rental Adjustment Clause (TRAC) Lease: Under a TRAC lease you would make a small down payment and at the end of the lease you'll have the option to purchase the truck for its residual value or have the leasing company sell the truck and you profit the difference or pay the loss.
- Lease purchase plans: These are for those of you who don't have enough for a down payment or have bad credit, but you would typically pay more than you would with traditional financing.

9. Let's build up your business

Every step or the way DAT solutions can help you grow your trucking business. Let DAT authority simplify getting operating authority and complying with government regulations.

DAT Load Boards – DAT solutions also maintains the largest and best load boards in North America that are helpful when you're searching for freights. Post your truck for fright brokers to call you and search nationwide for loads.

Freight Rates – DAT load boards can also be helpful if you're not sure how much to charge. The load board packages will include current market rates.

DAT fuel card – this will save you on fuel costs at over 1,900 truck stops all over the country.

Freight factoring – DAT has partnered with OTR Capital to provide a service that allows you to increase your cashflow without using debt.

Drug Testing – Use experts to get fast and reliable results when drug testing to navigate the complicated system that regulates this area of your business.

ATBS – DAT Trucker is a free mobile app that helps truckers find the nearest truck stops, rest areas, service stations, Walmart, or trucker friendly hotels. This app is also useful to find loads available to you based on your location, it saves you time and money with tax and accounting services, and bookkeeping.

Carrier TMS – You can get help managing your operations with AXEL TMS. This system gives you total control to manage your operations such as ELDs, load boards, and accounting with the click of a button.

CHAPTER EIGHTEEN

HOW TO WRITE A BOOK – 15 STEPS

1. What is your big idea?

One thing that is essential to getting past the first page of your first draft is an idea.

2. What genre is your book in?

Now that you have your big idea, do you know what genre you're in? When you're researching your genre, the best way to learn how to write in a certain genre is going to be reading books within that genre. You're already ahead of the game if you're trying to write a book in a genre that you like to read.

3. Now you can create an outline.

All great stories start with a solid outline, but this is especially important for your first book. This outline is the blueprint for you to rely on when you get stuck in the writing process.

*** Peep Game* When you have so many types of outlines, pick one that works for you. Your options include a free-flowing mind map, the rigorous chapter and scene outline, the character-based outline, and so on. Having a loose plan is better than not having a plan at all. Ensure that you have a beginning, middle, and end to your story because a lot of authors go into writing a book with a strong notion of how their story should start only.**

4. Start off strong

Get into the actual writing and make a dent in your first draft. Starting the story is going to be one of the most important parts of writing a book. It's no exaggeration to say your first few pages can make or break your book – If these pages aren't good enough, many readers will lose interest, possibly never returning to your book again.

***Peep Game* First off you need an opening hook that grabs the reader's attention and makes it impossible for them to look away.**

5. Focus on substance

It's common for writers to believe that the secret to writing an amazing book is the style, such as elaborate sentences, extensive vocabulary, and figurative language that even Shakespeare would like. It's true, style is great, but substance is far more important when you're writing a book.

6. Write "reader first"

Write a book that people will enjoy and buy. This is pretty much the cardinal rule: you should always be thinking about your audience and trying to write "reader first".

7. Set word count goals

Using word count goals is crucial to your writing process, especially when you're trying to finish your book in a certain amount of time. You should set and monitor your goals on a monthly and weekly basis.

I recommend the following word count goals:

- 500-750 words per day
- 1,500-2,500 words per week
- 6,000-10,000 words per month

These goals are based on a pattern of 3-4 sessions per week, which is reasonable for a beginner, but still enough to make commendable progress, even if you only follow out minimum recommendations - 500 words per session at 3 sessions per week you can still easily finish your book in less than a year.

Speeding up the writing process - If you are looking for how to write a book as fast as possible, your word count goals should look a little more like this:

- 1,500-2,000 words per session
- 9,000-15,000 words per week
- 35,000-50,000 words per month

It's hard work but it's really possible.

8. Establish a healthy routine

By having a healthy routine, you can reach your word count goals faster and have a better experience with writing overall. Start out by asking yourself some questions to help you establish a healthy routine.

- When are you the freest in the day or week?
- What is the most productive time of day for you?
- Is this realistic for you to balance these goals with your other responsibilities?

***Peep Game* The best way to set up your routine is to take advantage of your pre-existing schedule and natural patterns.**

9. Set up a productive space

Another major component of how to write a book is where you write. You're only going to be able to complete an entire book if you can find a calm and focused space to do your writing.

10. Use writing software such as

Scrivener
Milanote
Focus Writer
The Reedsy book editor

11. Keep yourself motivated

Finding your flow with writing a book can be challenging but here are a few motivational strategies for you to try:

- Make a list of reasons why you want to write a book
- Find someone else to write with you
- Reward yourself at important milestones

12. Take setbacks as they come

There are countless ways to overcome writers block, from freewriting to working on your characters to taking a shower. Here are some of the most effective techniques I found:

- Revisit your outline
- Try writing exercises
- Share your experience with friends
- Take a break and try to do something else

Most importantly remember that setbacks are going to happen so take them in stride and don't let it get you down.

13. Don't rush the ending

Ending a book is not an easy task, and poor third act plotting is one of the most common authorial pitfalls.

14. Get tons of feedback

You can write all day, all night, to your hearts content… but if no one else likes what you've written, you might end up heartbroken instead. That's why it's crucial to request feedback on your book, starting early and from as many sources as possible.

15. Publish your book

You made it to the end, finally; you've brainstormed, written your outline, written your first draft and spent extensive time editing it after getting feedback. Now that you couldn't be prouder, your book is in its final form. What's the next step? Publish your book…

CHAPTER NINETEEN

HOW TO START A NIGHTCLUB

To be successful as an entrepreneur you have to have a clear plan. This is going to layout the plan for the specifics of your business as well as discover some of the unknowns. Here are some things that you're gonna have to think about:

- What are the startup and ongoing costs?
- Who is your target market?
- How much can you charge customers?
- What will you name your business?

Here are some things that I found:

What are the costs involved in opening a night club? If you don't have the money to buy a club right now the best way to get going is to make a deal with an established night club as a promoter who hosts certain nights of the month, or week depending on popularity. Clubs can charge you a minimum bar cost that you have to pay for the night, so you could lose money if nobody shows up, but this is a good way to see if you're able to attract a crowd with your ideas for parties.

***Peep Game* You might want to rethink getting into this business if you can't attract a crowd for one night.**

The second-best way is to purchase an established club that is already successful. For this opportunity will pay you back at lease 10 times the annual profits to buy the club, not counting the real estate if it's included.

Starting up a new club has costs that vary depending on where it's located. A ballpark number for this could be around $100,000 depending on fixtures, supplies, and equipment need to get you started. Other clubs, like the largest clubs in New York City can cost tens of millions of dollars to open.

The basic equipment needed is:

• Refrigerators - $1,000 standalone style to $10,000 walk in style
• Freezers - $2,000 standalone style to $20,000 walk in style
• Bottle Coolers - $1,000 each
• Bar Coolers - $1,500 each
• Under bar sink - $900 each
• Draft beer equipment - $500 per station
• Equipment to make soda - $300 for each station
• Ice machine - $2,500 each
• Glass racks/speed rails - $200 each
• Glass washing machine - $1,400 each
• Bar blender - $250 each
• Various sized glassware - $25 per 24 glasses
• Bar - $4,000-$10,000
• Bar stools - $75 each
• Bar lighting - $1,000 each
• Bar Supplies – utensils, condiments, etc. - $300
• Soda, beer, and liquor stock inventory - $10,000 - $50,000 (Replaced daily as used)

What are the ongoing expenses for a night club? If you're offering food then you can add that cost to your ongoing expenses, along with labor cost, beverage cost, rent, utilities, marketing, and insurance.

Who is the target market? Your best customers are going to have a lot of money and want to spend it on a wild night out. Big spenders like this can make a club very profitable, this can attract famous people who naturally attract others.

How does a nightclub make money? To make money in your nightclub you're going to be selling drinks, maybe food, charging admission, and where you can special seating/services that you can offer to customers. Special services can be anything from bottle service, where customers purchase a full bottle of liquor at a VIP table, all the way up to a lap dance.

How much can you charge customer? Some drinks can sell as low as $1 per glass for cheap beer or a shot of cheap liquor up to hundreds of dollars for a bottle of fine wine, expensive champagne, and "top shelf" alcohol. In the main American cities, the average drink sale $2.50 for a beer and $5.00 for liquor drinks. Your blended drinks can sell for around $10 each.

***Peep Game* Sometimes clubs can charge a cover charge to get in the club, typically $5-$10 per person but this money is used to help pay the bands and/or performance events which, due to limited seating/capacity, can sell out.**

How much profit can a nightclub make? Typically, smaller clubs bring in around $1,000 to $5,000 each week, or $50,000 to $250,000 per week. The largest nightclubs can make easily make $50,000 in a single night.

How can you make your business more profitable? Hosting a variety of events to get your clubs name out there as well as some sideline businesses related to your club such as:

- Comedy night
- Live music
- Open Mic/Karaoke night
- Private parties
- Record audio and video of the band's performance

10 Steps

1. Create a plan
2. Form a legal entity
3. Register for taxes
4. Open your bank account and credit cards
5. Set up business accounting
6. Obtain necessary permits and licenses
7. Get business insurance
8. Define your brand
9. Create your business website
10. Set up your business phone system

Chapter Twenty

How to start a record label

1. Create a plan
2. Form a legal entity
3. Register to pay taxes
4. Open your bank account and a credit card
5. Set up business accounting
6. Obtain necessary permits and licenses
7. Get business insurance
8. Define your brand
9. Create your business website
10. Make/Sell music

What are the costs of starting a record label?

Recording – This is anywhere between zero and $15,000 or more, if you're looking to produce a record at a commercial sound studio then you're looking at hundreds of dollars per hour. If this if the route you choose then you're going to want to maximize your time in the studio by being well-rehearsed. Sometimes audio engineers or music producers can enter the field of owning a label and begin with recording the talent in their own commercial or at-home studios. Some others may only work with artists who've already recorded their work and focus more on marketing and distribution of the music, avoiding recording costs altogether.

Graphic design – many hundreds of dollars, on up. This includes the costs of the label's logo design and the look of your first product.

Manufacturing – about $1.2 per unit for CDs and $5 or $6 or more for vinyl.

Many labels are solely releasing digital music these days due to the rising costs of pressing music.

Entertaining, Networking – several hundred dollars a year or more. Often, you're going to want to be attending shows and hanging out with talent, which brings the cost of tickets, drinks, travel, and other recruitment costs. If you're looking all over the country for this talent, or even internationally, these costs can rise considerably.

Promotion – usually this is a few thousand dollars. A lot of labels will increase awareness by using a publicist, music promoters, booking agents to impact record sales, radio play, and ticket sales for your live shows.

Legal services - $500 - $1,000. You can find an artist contract template online but you're better off enlisting professional guidance in writing at least your first contract.

What are ongoing expenses for a record label?

The biggest ongoing expenses you're going to have been going to be the costs for pressing new physical units and promoting new releases. A lot of your other costs will show in a percentage of your sales, for example the cut you pay your artist, composer, or distributor.

Who is the target market?

Use the bars, clubs, and other performance venues around you to research who your customers are in terms of age, education, and lifestyle. All of these things are going to help you determine how to target and speak to your audience.

How does a record label make money?

Today you can buy music through a variety of digital physical channels. Fans buy vinyl records, compact discs, MP3 files, and streams from websites such as Spotify. In addition, labels can earn money through licensing deals involving use of the music soundtracks in film and television and in commercials and video games and other commercial outlets. Other income can be generated through digital and satellite transmissions like Sirius radio. And finally, some indie labels sign their talents to what's called 360 deals. In which the label takes a revenue split for booking the talent in live shows, selling t-shirts, and other merchandise and generating other associated income streams.

How much can you charge customers?

Prices are pretty much determined by the market. Vinyl records generally sell for $18 or $20, while compact discs sell for a bit less. Streaming services such as Spotify might pay a fraction of a penny per play and iTunes downloads might sell for $7 or $10 for an album or a dollar for a single. With how high the cost of manufacturing and packaging your physical units, you as the label may only make a dollar per unit once the manufacturer, artist, composer, and publisher are paid. With digital platforms such as iTunes the label and your talent can snag at least half the cost of the download.

How much profit can a record label make?

Consider XL recordings, the small British indie label that discovered and released music for the likes of Adele, Radiohead, Vampire Weekend, and other popular big names, selling millions of units in the process. With how much things can be streamed or downloaded, almost 40 percent of the music today is produced by indies. Which greatly reduces physical material costs. Theoretically distribution is easier online as well. The downside of all that potential is how many others are out there for you to compete with. Many indie labels only sell a few hundred units, and a lot of the business is conducted on a part time basis.

How can you make your business more profitable?

Consider producing compilation albums as samples of your label's artist roster. Also, looking into working with other indie labels to record music and consult the distribution of their output. And finally, get the full involvement and sell records and merch at shows.

CHAPTER TWENTY-ONE

HOW TO START A RESTAURANT

Have you thought about what all of the costs involved with opening a restaurant are going to be?

The overall costs to opening a restaurant can vary, but generally include:

- Building security deposit: $10,000- $12,000
- First month's rent: $10,000 to $15,000
- First month's utilities: $2,500
- Customized build out for the kitchen: up to $350,000
- Tables and furniture: $40,000-$50,000
- Initial overhead including food and prep materials: $8,000-$15,000
- POS: $1,500-$20,000
- Insurance: Up to $6,000
- Sign: $10,000-$20,000
- Menu printouts: $1,500
- Business Cards: $70 to $300
- Flyers: $5,000 to $10,000
- Grand Opening event: $15,000
- PR for Grand Opening: $5,000

***Peep Game* You can expect to be looking towards $600,000 depending on the type of restaurant you want to run. You can increase or decrease these costs depending on many factors including your location, equipment, and any vendors you need to purchase essentials through.**

What are the ongoing expenses for a restaurant? Restaurants have many expenses that are ongoing, but the major ones include:

• Depending on your location the rent can be anywhere from $10,000 to $12,000.
• Utilities, which can include phone, internet, electricity, water, gas: up to $2,500 per month (sometimes more depending on location)
• Depending on your menu the food and supplies can cost $10,000 to $15,000, or more.
• Labor cost: this varies based on staff needs.

Who is the target market? Your customers are individuals or groups/families who are dining out for the day or evening. Some restaurants will also do catering for large events with business or government organizations, birthdays, and other larger scale events.

How does a restaurant make money? Restaurants are making their money by charging customers for food and drinks they have prepared for them. Prices are typically fixed on a menu. It's also encouraged for customers to tip the waitstaff for good or exceptional service. For wait staff, tipping is customary. Sometimes these tips are gathered and split amongst workers in the restaurant, or they contribute to the waitstaffs' pay.

How much can you charge customers? The pricing on your menu can vary considerably just based on the type of restaurant and food being served. For example, when you're at a high-end restaurant that serves seafood, you can see prices between $20 and $50 per plate. A small diner may charge between $4 and $10 a plate.

How much profit can a restaurant make? This industry has a high rate of failure but the businesses that do make it can also be extremely successful. Even a modest operation can turn over $1 million or more in revenue in a year based on location and the type of restaurant.

How can you make your business more profitable? A more profitable restaurant is one that usually targets a specific demographic or narrows its cuisine to service a specific type of market.

What will you name your business? Choosing the right name is important and challenging if you don't already have a name in mind, come up with different names and ideas also google them to make sure no one else has them.

CONGRATULATIONS

First and foremost, I would like to thank you for purchasing this book. If you are reading this congratulations, you have made it to the end. Unlike many of your peers you are destined to win in life no matter what your current circumstances are. When I first made a commitment to write this book, I thought of you first. I wanted to breakdown various topics on business, marketing, bank accounts, credit cards, etc. I wanted to make this language as simple as it gets in order for you to understand and grasp each concept. A lot of us were born enTRAPreneurs with a hustler's spirit, but in this book I show you many ways to get money legally. We have to think of longevity in order to stay in this game and win. My intentions on writing this book were to give you some knowledge and information that could help you become a better and more successful person.

Do you want to become rich? Of course, you do! Why wait until tomorrow to be successful? Here I give you tons of information that you can use to live your dreams today. You no longer have to hustle harder, this is your opportunity to hustle smarter! This book the enTRAPreneur is your everything guide to financial freedom. There is no time to waste. Time is money and money is time. Become richer today! You have discovered not only riches but also financial intelligence! Once again, I thank you and remember you too are a rich prisoner. GET MONEY!

The Richest Prisoner

About The Author

Keiko "O.G.Kayko" Thomas is The Richest Prisoner in America and an incarcerated author who has published Aaron Hernandez: the untold prison story and a follow up of over 4 other titles. He is the Founder,Chairman, and CEO of Penitentiary Rich, LLC and Inmate Link, Inc. He specialize in fiction and non fiction,but mostly self help, how to books,and prison culture. He is also an artist/ entertainer,motivational speaker, and life coach who slogan "Its up 2 you" has become something that the prisoner community hold fast to.

Contact O.G. Kayko @

Keiko Thomas # W108727
SBCC
Po Box 8000
Shirley,Ma 01464

fb/Instagram @ O.G.Kayko

Our Current Titles:

www.penitentiaryrich.com and Amazon

All payments are accepted at wwwpententiaryrich.com and Amazon
We accept Institutional checks at:
PO BOX 860037
Plano, TX 75086

$19.99

Aaron Hernandez: The Untold Prison Story

In this book, the author gives you a closer look at Aaron Hernandez aka Double-A. He brings Double-A to the light and pushes Aaron Hernandez to the shadows. This author reveals conversations between him and the former New England Patriot. This is the closest you get! From walks in the prison yard, selling & using drugs, to playing basketball. From prison politics to talks about Tom Brady, the Great. This is the inside scoop you have been waiting for.

Thinking Rich, Living Broke

$4.99

This is a motivational booklet for those who are seeking success. These 7 chapters are filled with inspirational words that gives you that spark to get up and become something greater. This booklet touches on every aspect og success from thinking rich to securing your future. If you are seeking something greater and want to become successful this booklet is for you. A must read.
Start thinking RICH NOW!

$9.99

Touched By Love

Touched by love is an incarcerated father's gift to his daughters. Not able to be there in the physical for them he wanted to make sure they grow to be strong, beautiful, intelligent, and independent women. He wrote them 15 principles to apply to their life and character. Even while incarcerated this father has given his daughters a gift that's forever lasting. After reading this book from beginning to end I hope you too become.

The Funny Truth

$19.99

This book is a collection of 25 short stories all about what I been through or seen. I wrote these stories in segregation (the hole) on pieces of brown napkins and just about any paper I could find. I decided to share only 25 of my best and favorite stories. These stories were written from my memory and designed to make you laugh. Also written to give you a glimpse at my life, and the things that I have been through or seen. Inside these pages I tell you, the reader, to laugh with me or at me because I don't care. I just want to make you smile. Smiling is good and it makes you feel better. Please Excuse my grammar and know that to change it would be to change the stories. So, no editorial needed. Please enjoy this book as well as I enjoyed writing it.

The EnTRAPreneur: A Beginners Guide to Success

If you have ever felt overwhelmed, confused, or intimidated by the world of enTRAPreneurship, this friendly book is your first step towards becoming a savvy, money-wise enTRAPreneur. In this fully updated book enTRAPreneur and Self-made Millionaire Keiko "O.G.Kayko" Thomas explains in simple language the intricacies of many different types of businesses, breakdowns, and much needed how to information.

$24.99

Frequently Asked Questions

Q: If I publish my work through you can I keep all my exclusive rights?
A: Yes and no. When you first publish with us, we will own all exclusive rights to the book/work, but later you can purchase all your rights back and will have permission to do so as you please.

Q: How long do I have to wait to purchase my rights back?
A: Our contracts vary but our standard is to reach out after one-year to discuss your options to purchase your rights back.

Q: Can I set the price for my book?
A: We welcome suggestions regarding the price but if it doesn't align with the backend process and cost then it would be subject to change, we have the final decision.

Q: How much can I make from each sale?
A: Here at Penitentiary Rich, we pay our authors a 30% royalty rate off each sale. That sale and rate is due to the cover price. For example: your book is priced at $10, and your percentage is 30% so 30% of $10.00 is $3.00. You would see $3.00 off each sale.

Q: Can I design my book cover?
A: Yes, absolutely it's your book you can do as you please, we're here to bring your vision to life. We also have professional cover designers that can work with you.

Q: Can I receive free copies of my book?
A: Yes, we will give you five free author copies.

Q: Can I purchase additional author copies?
Yes, we charge $3.50 per book, the order limit cannot exceed 999 at a time.

Q: How does the author's advanced pay work?
A: The author advanced pay is tailored to your contract. When these contracts are put into place you would be eligible for the advanced pay once all completed copies of the required works have been received and approved. Keep in mind that all advanced pay is recouped completely before the first royalty payment will be paid out. Royalties are paid out 60-90 days from the date of the sale and only get dispersed when the payment is above $50.

Q: How do I get a book deal and contract with Penitentiary Rich?
A: All you have to do is reach out to us through the postal mail or email.

Penitentiary Rich, LLC
PO BOX 860037
Plano, TX 75086
chiefeditor@penitentiaryrich.com

Q: Does my manuscript have to be typed?
A: Absolutely not. All you have to do is write it. We will help you bring whatever your vision is to life.

Q: How do you promote and market?
A: We promote and market using various sources such as social media marking with Facebook and Instagram, pay-per-click ads with Amazon and Google. We also promote through magazine ads and our website.

Q: Can I write up my own promotion or press release?
A: Absolutely, just write and send it to us.

We publish all kinds of material. We are not like other publishing companies that muzzle their authors. We give our authors freedom to write and create. All you have to do is write it. We don't charge our authors for packages or none of that!! Really just write and we will do all the work.

Submission Guidelines:

- A Cover or Query letter
- A complete summary/synopsis/overview
- Authors information sheet (This should include a bio and background)
- Three sample chapters

We ask that you do not send the originals but if that is the only option please be sure to include that so we can make a copy and send it back to you.

Made in the USA
Monee, IL
05 November 2026

67816248R00049